Revise your Sounds

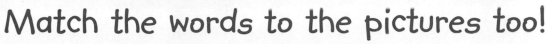

CAN YOU Remember these sounds from Activity Books 1, 2, 3, 4, 5 and 6?

Tick the sounds and words that you can read!

Match the words to the pictures too! ✓

s v n oa or w e t a

b p

ck sh

ie l

h g

ch th

ng j

ai f

y d

sheep

corn

snail

frog

Tricky Words

The   I

u z x i o ee m oo r

qu

Inky, Bee and Snake are visiting a wildlife park. "Look at all those ducks," buzzes Bee. "I didn't know there were so many different kinds - "qu, qu, qu!" she quacks at them. "I want to see the rest of the animals now," hisses Snake in a croaky voice. "Are you all right?" asks Inky. "I think so," says Snake, coughing. "You sound like a strange duck when you cough!" says Bee.

Colour the picture!

NOW YOU CAN
Do the action and say the sound!

Action
Make a duck's beak with your hands, and say *qu, qu, qu.*

Which of these things have the sound 'qu' in them? Join them to the 'qu'.

Inky says, "Hold your pencil correctly!"

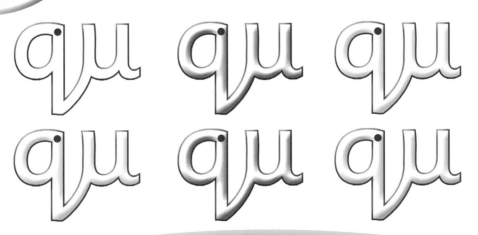

Tips for Parents
When joining 'q' and 'u', write the 'q' as usual, then bring the joining tail up to start the 'u'.

Quiz Questions

NOW YOU CAN

Answer yes or no to these quick questions!

Can ducks quack? | yes | no |

I sleep in a bed. | yes | no |

Is a snail quick? | yes | no |

A cat has kittens. | yes | no |

Can fish swim? | yes | no |

Can dogs sing? | yes | no |

What's Your Name?

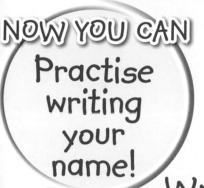

Write your first name here.

Would you like to try writing your surname here?

Try different colours!

Tips for Parents

If your child finds this tricky, use tracing paper and ask them to trace their name.

ou

Inky, Bee and Snake walk past the owl house until they reach the porcupines. Most of them are asleep but outside, two porcupines are looking angrily at each other. "Look at the spikes on those!" Bee gasps. "They're called needles, not spikes," says Snake. "I wouldn't want any of those needles stuck into me - ou, ou, ou!" shudders Bee.

Colour the picture!

NOW YOU CAN
Do the action and say the sound!

Action
Pretend your finger is a needle and prick your thumb, saying *OU, OU, OU.*

Which of these things have the sound 'ou' in them?
Join them to the 'ou'.

NOW YOU CAN
Write the letters. Start at the top and join the letters.

Inky says, "Try writing joined letters!"

ou ou ou ou

ou ou ou

 Tips for Parents
When joining 'o' and 'u', write the 'o' as usual, then go straight across to where the 'u' starts.

Sticker Activity

NOW YOU CAN
Read the words and find the stickers that match.

Put your stickers on the porcupines.

cloud

shout

house

round

mouth

mouse

hound

south

NOW YOU CAN
Find the mouse sticker with the vowel sound to match the picture on the house.

Sticker Activity

PUT THE MOUSE IN ITS HOUSE

The first one is done for you!

oi

Next day, Inky suggests they go boating on the lake. They each climb into a small boat and set off into the middle of the lake, towards the islands. As she rounds the end of the first island, Bee sees Snake rowing off towards the next one. "oi!" Bee calls, "oi! Over here!" She jumps up and waves, nearly falling into the lake.

Colour the picture!

SNACKS

TOILETS

NOW YOU CAN

Do the action and say the sound!

Action
Cup your hands around your mouth and pretend to shout at a passing boat, saying *Oi! Ship ahoy!*

Which of these things have the sound 'oi' in them?
Join them to the 'oi'.

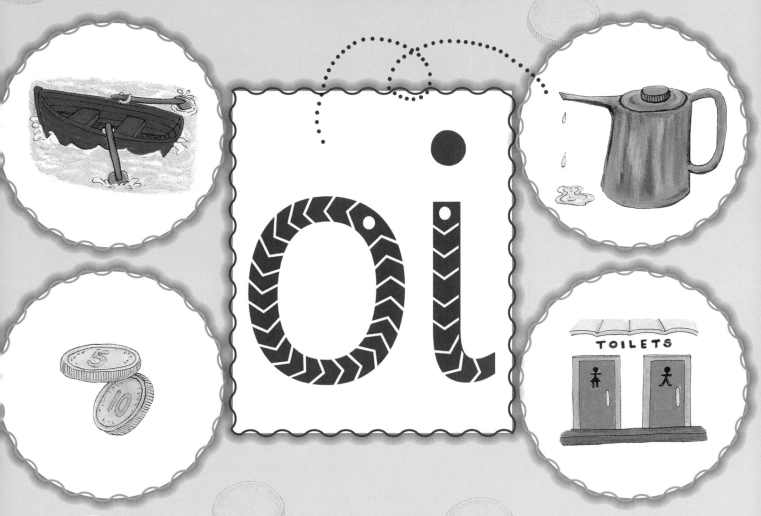

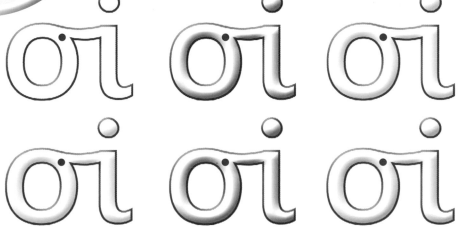

oi oi oi

oi oi oi

Inky says, "Hold your pencil correctly!"

💡 **Tips for Parents**
When joining 'o' and 'i', write the 'o' as usual, then go straight across to where the 'i' starts.

Sticker Activity

COIN MAZE

Help Bee to fly around the island and read the words. For each word you can read, place a coin sticker over the top. How many coins have you collected by the time you reach Snake's money box?

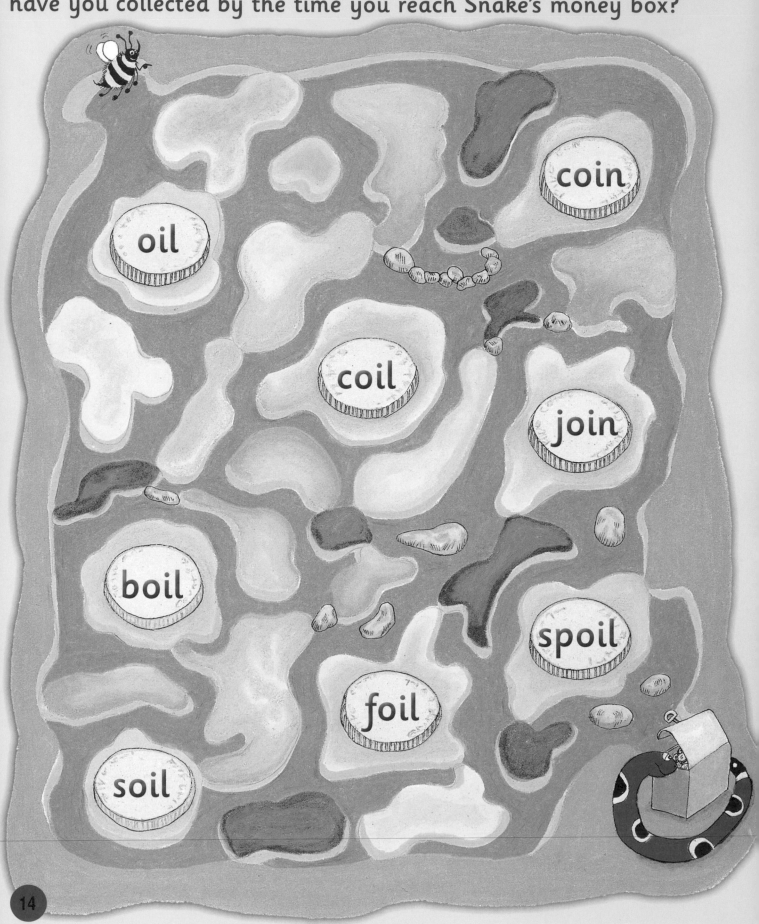

animal anagrams

Can you unscramble the animal names and write them underneath?

g d o

_ _ _

t a b

_ _ _

a k y

_ _ _

i sh f

_ _ _

ck d u

_ _ _ _

oa d t

_ _ _ _

b c r a

_ _ _ _

p a d a n

_ _ _ _ _

o p t a rr

_ _ _ _ _ _

ue

A little while later, Bee darts off into a clump of trees shouting, "Bet you can't find me!" Snake and Inky hurry after her and look around. Then Snake spots Bee's wings sticking out from behind a tree. "I see you - ue, ue!" he shouts, pointing his tail to where Bee is hiding.

Colour the picture!

BBQ MENU
HOT DOGS
HAMBURGERS
VEGGIE BURGER
JUICE

JUICE JUICE

NOW YOU CAN
Do the action and say the sound!

Action
Point to people around you and say *you, you, you.*

Which of these things have the sound 'ue' in them?
Join them to the 'ue'.

NOW YOU CAN
Write the letters. Start on the dot and join the letters.

Inky says, "Hold your pencil correctly!"

ue ue ue

ue ue ue

💡 **Tips for Parents**
When joining 'u' and 'e', write the 'u' as usual, then take the joining tail up to start the 'e'.

TRICKY WORD HAT POSTER

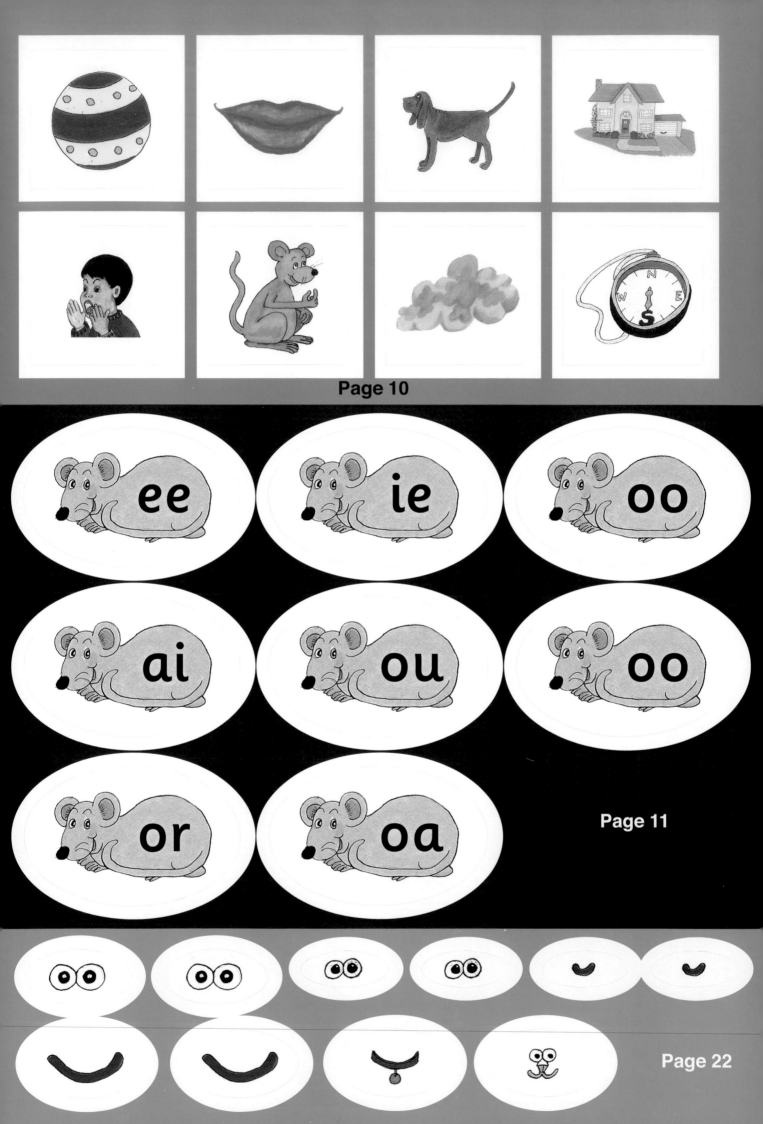

Page 10

Page 11

Page 22

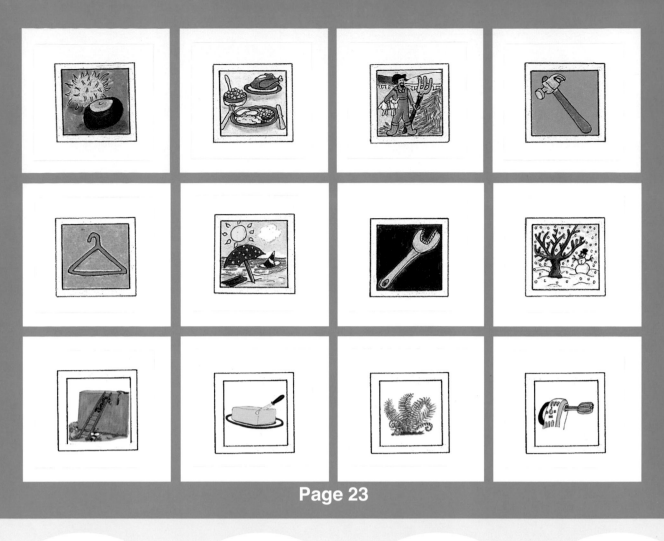

Page 23

Page 14

Page 22

NOW YOU CAN

Read the tricky words, cut them out, and match them to the words on the plant opposite.

he

be

me

to

the

do

she

was

we

I

Cut out the flowers carefully!

er

Inky, Bee and Snake find a good spot to sit down and watch the otters whilst they are eating their picnic lunch. "Goody!" exclaims Bee. "You've brought the gingerbread we made yesterday. I enjoyed using the mixer, *erererer*, to make them." Perhaps we can make some otter shapes next time!" says Inky.

Colour the picture!

NOW YOU CAN
Do the action and say the sound!

Action
Roll your hands over each other, like a mixer, and say *er-er-er-er*.

Which of these things have the sound 'er' in them? Join them to the 'er'.

NOW YOU CAN
Write the letters. Start on the dot and join the letters.

Inky says, "Start at the dot!"

er er er

er er er

💡 **Tips for Parents**
When joining 'e' and 'r', write the 'e' as usual, then take the joining tail up to start the 'r'.

Decorate the Gingerbread Family

Colour them first!

Now add detail using the stickers!

How to make your own gingerbread family

Ingredients: 2oz butter, 6oz self-raising flour, ½ tsp bicarbonate of soda, 1½ tbsp syrup, 1tsp ginger, icing for decorating.

Put the oven on gas mark 5 (375 F°). Melt the butter, syrup and sugar. Sift the flour, ginger and bicarbonate of soda. Stir the flour mix into the butter, syrup and sugar until it becomes a stiff dough. Roll it out and use cutters to cut it into gingerbread shapes. Place in the oven for 10 mins.

Stamps!

Read the word on the envelope and then find the stamp sticker to match. Remember that if two letters that make the same sound come together, you only need to say it once.

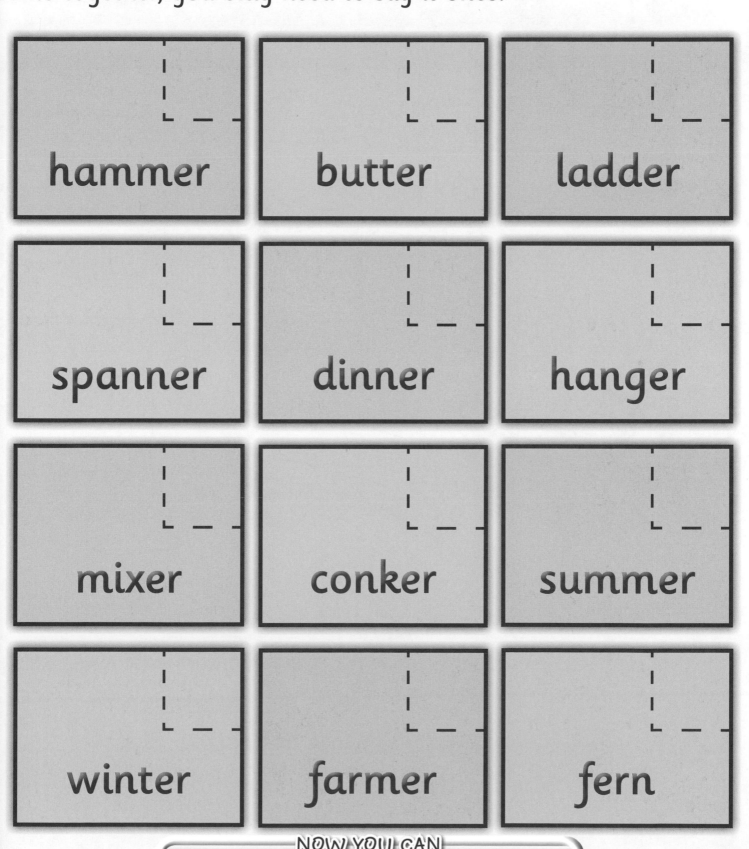

hammer

butter

ladder

spanner

dinner

hanger

mixer

conker

summer

winter

farmer

fern

NOW YOU CAN
Stick the stamp stickers on the letters!

ar

Inky, Snake and Bee look at the aardvarks and the armadillos, and then watch the sea lions for a while. A big sea lion on the rocks barks, "ar, ar, ar". Snake's voice is getting more and more croaky. Inky tells Snake to open his mouth so she can look at his throat. "Say, 'ar!'," says Inky. "ar!" says Snake, obediently. "You sound like that sea lion," laughs Bee.

Colour the picture!

SEE OATS

← SHARKS

Armadillos

NOW YOU CAN

Do the action and say the sound!

Action
Open your mouth and say *ah.*

Which of these things have the sound 'ar' in them?
Join them to the 'ar'.

NOW YOU CAN

Write the letters. Start on the dot and join the letters.

Inky says, "Try writing joined letters!"

ar ar ar

ar ar ar

💡 **Tips for Parents**
When joining 'a' and 'r', write the 'a' as usual, then take the joining tail up to start the 'r'.

CAR PARK

Can you park the cars in the right spaces?
Cut out the cars at the bottom of the page and stick them
in the right spaces in the car park.

art	scarf	car	start
barn	card	farm	yard
star	park	sharp	dark

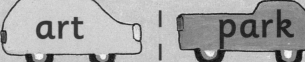

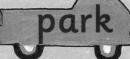 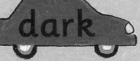 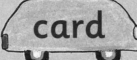 

farm — art — park — car

barn — dark — card — yard

star — sharp — scarf — start

ON THE FARM

Read the word in each pen or field
and draw a picture of it.

Colour
the
farm!

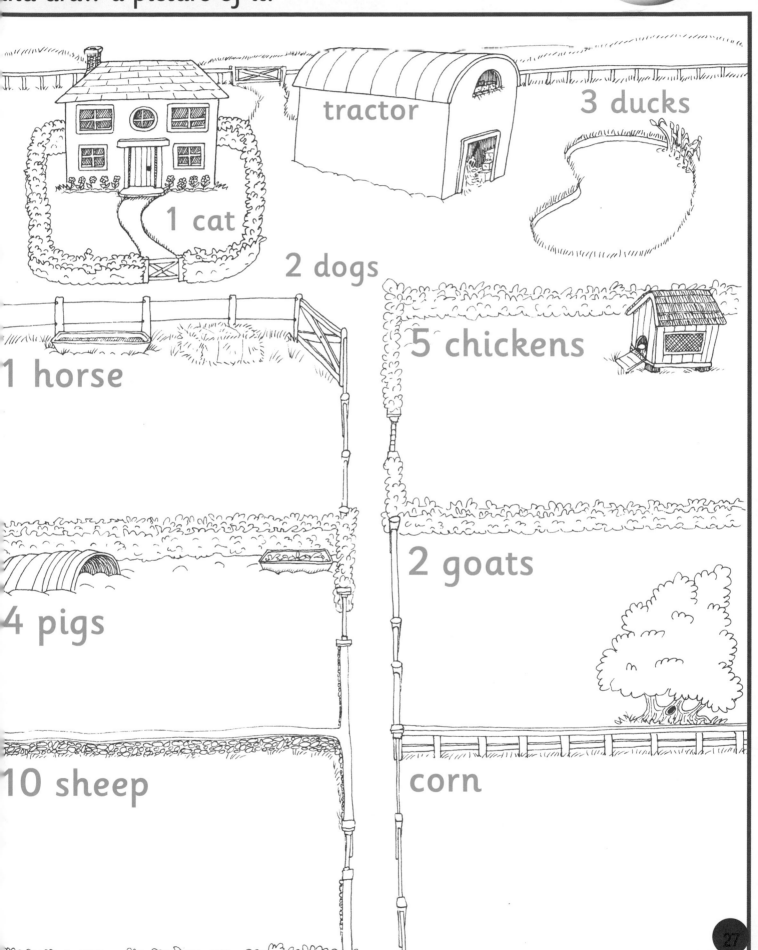

tractor

3 ducks

1 cat

2 dogs

5 chickens

1 horse

2 goats

4 pigs

10 sheep

corn

Sound Cards

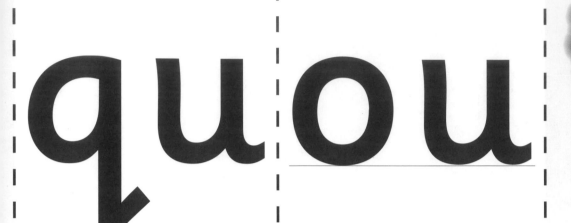

qu ou

oi ue

er ar

Tips for Parents

Cut out each card and use them in the ways suggested. Keep them and add them to the sound cards in the other activity books.

28

NOW YOU CAN

Write over the dotted letters, then read the sentences.

This is Moat Farm.

I can see a cat.

I can see 2 dogs.

The dogs are Ben

and Neb.

Start each letter on the large dot!

Word and Picture Matching

NOW YOU CAN Join the words to the pictures and later you can cut out and match.

cap

pen

hip

cat

quilt

coin

mouth

statue

 30

More Word and Picture Matching

letter	
arm	
fern	
cloud	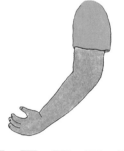
shark	
queen	

31

MORE TRICKY WORDS

he she

Remember, some words are tricky and can't be sounded out.

NOW YOU CAN
Have a go at writing these tricky words.

Try to stay inside the lines!

he he he he he

he he he he he

she she she she she

she she she she she

TRICKY WORD SENTENCES

Read the sentences and draw pictures to show you understand what you have read.

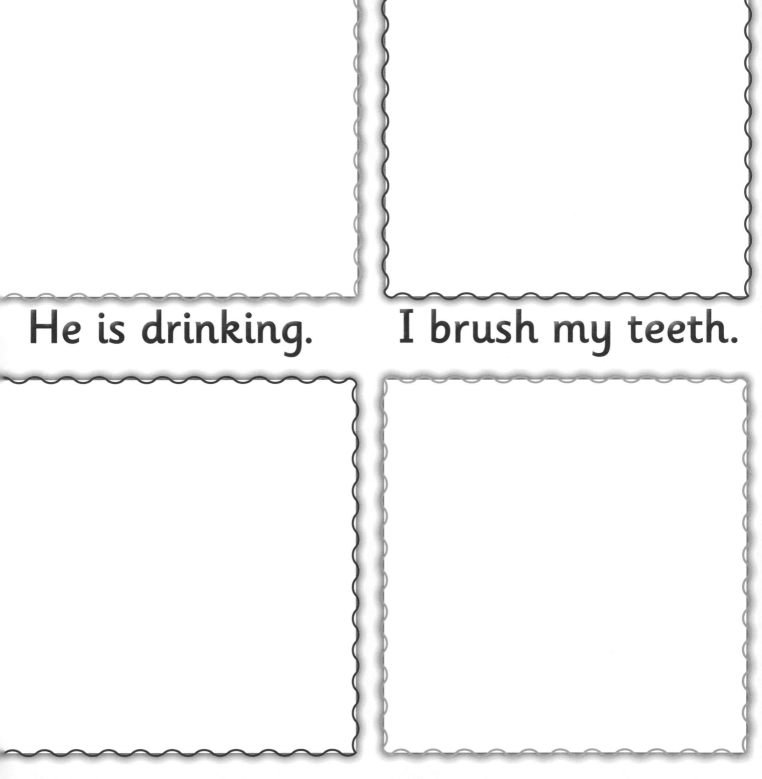

He is drinking.

I brush my teeth.

She is running.

The dog is spotty.

Practise Writing the Letters

Start on the dot and try to stay inside the lines!

qu qu qu qu

ou ou ou ou

oi oi oi oi

ue ue ue ue

er er er er

ar ar ar ar

34